BEAD LIGHTNING

SHEET LIGHTNING

FORK LIGHTNING

HEAT LIGHTNING

Up to 9
150

STREAK LIGHTNING

RIBBON LIGHTNING

BALL LIGHTNING

Also by John and Cathy Polgreen
A LOOK AT THE MOON

The authors thank Gerald L. Shak, Supervising Forecaster of the United States Weather Bureau Office, New York, for his help in checking the manuscript of this book.

THUNDER
AND
LIGHTNING

TEXT AND PICTURES

by JOHN AND CATHY POLGREEN

DOUBLEDAY & COMPANY, INC.

GARDEN CITY, NEW YORK

LIBRARY OF CONGRESS CATALOG CARD NUMBER: 63-7361. COPYRIGHT © 1963 BY JOHN AND CATHLEEN POLGREEN
ALL RIGHTS RESERVED. PRINTED IN THE UNITED STATES OF AMERICA.
FIRST EDITION

This is a thunderstorm. It is raining very hard.
You can see bright streaks of lightning. There is
a loud crash of thunder. Did you ever wonder
where a thunderstorm comes from?

A thunderstorm comes from a special kind of a cloud called a *thundercloud*. This is how a thundercloud usually forms.

It is late afternoon on a hot day. The air near the ground is warm. This air is also damp. The warm damp air quickly rises. It rises into the upper air which is always very cold. Now the warm air cools off. The dampness in this air turns into tiny drops of water. The millions of tiny drops form a small cloud. To us, the cloud looks white.

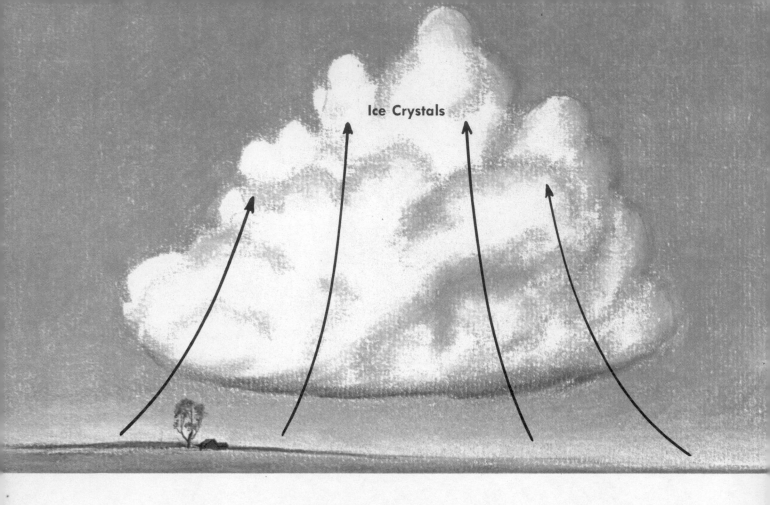

Ice Crystals

More dampness makes more and more water drops. The cloud grows bigger and bigger. It stretches higher and higher.

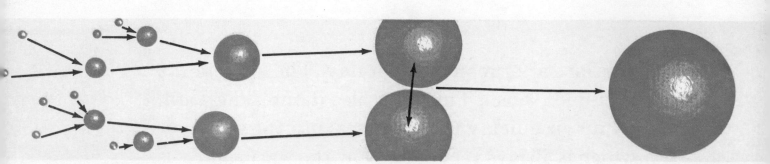

Some of the drops of water join together. They make bigger drops. Some of the water at the top of the cloud freezes into tiny ice crystals.

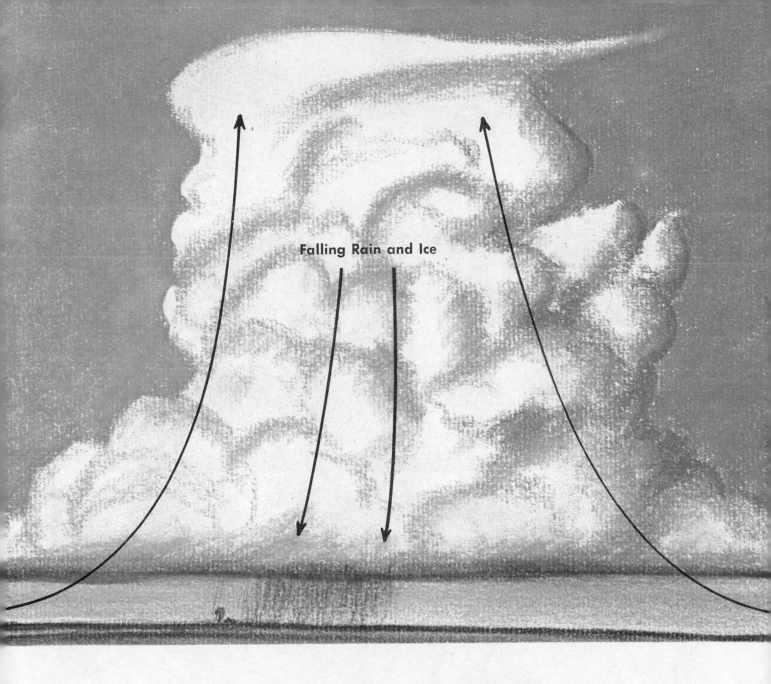

Falling Rain and Ice

Soon the raindrops and ice become too heavy for the air to hold up. Now the cloud is a full-grown thundercloud. The heavy rain and ice begin to fall out of the cloud and down to the ground. Usually the hail melts before it hits the ground. This is how the thundercloud looks from a distance.

When the thundercloud is above you, it looks very
thick and dark. It seems to cover the whole sky.

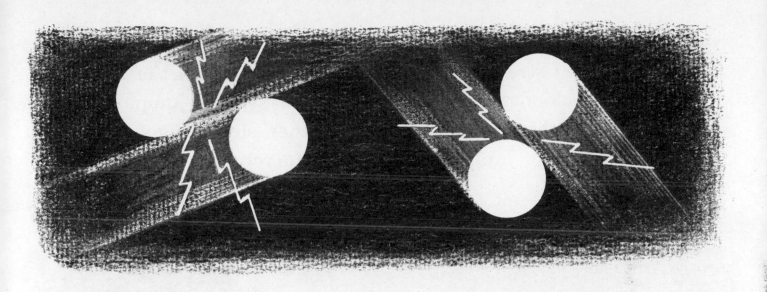

Inside of the cloud, all of the particles of air and water are rushing around. As they rub against each other, they make *electricity*. We can see some of the electricity flash through the sky like a giant spark. This flash is lightning.

Bright streaks of lightning jump from one part of the cloud to another part. Other streaks jump from the thundercloud to another cloud. Some lightning jumps from the thundercloud to the ground.

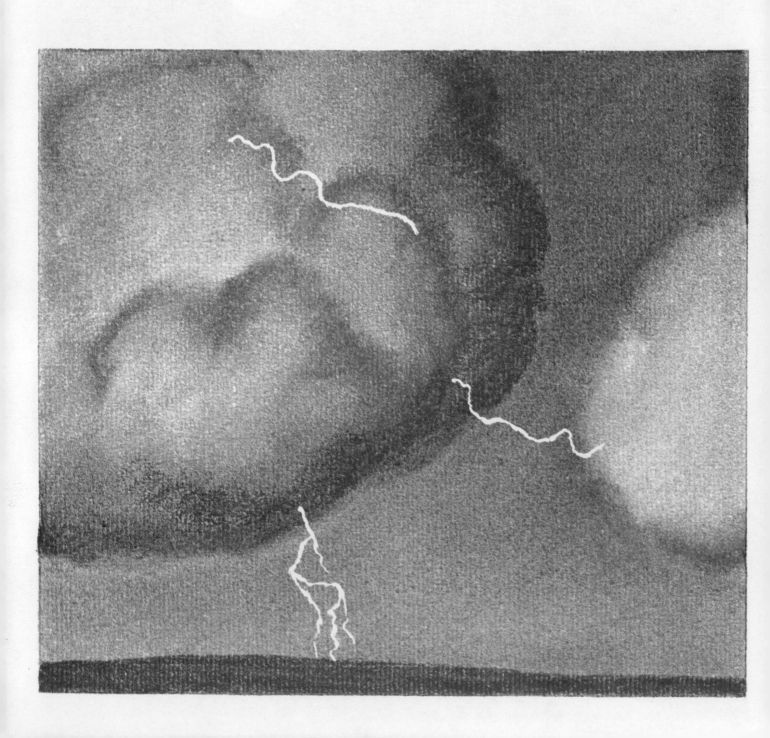

The electricity in a thundercloud is very much like the electricity in a lighted bulb. However, there is one big difference. We can push a button and turn the light bulb on and off. But we can't turn lightning on, and we can't turn lightning off.

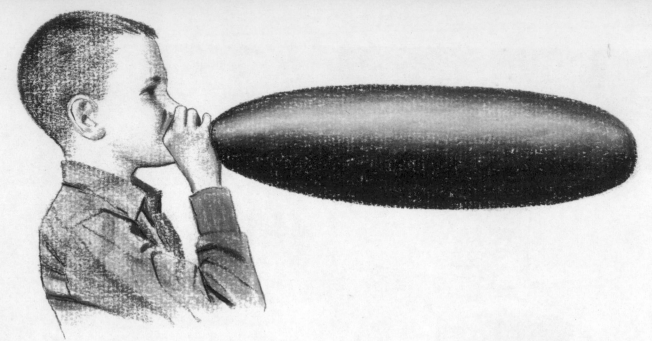

Each streak of lightning is followed by a noisy crash of thunder. In order to understand what makes the noise, let's first think about a balloon. If you blow and blow, you can squeeze a lot of air into a balloon. Now if you stick a pin in the balloon, the crowded air in the balloon rushes out with a loud bang.

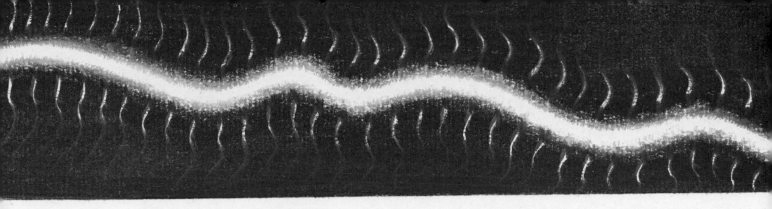

Thunder, too, is the sound of crowded air rushing to get to another place. As lightning streaks through the sky, it quickly heats up the air around it.

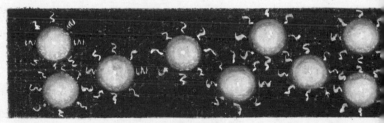

The heat enlarges the millions and millions of tiny specks of air.

As these specks enlarge, they crowd and bang against each other with a loud crash—a crash of thunder.

Sound travels through the air quite slowly. You can prove this the next time you are outdoors. Have a friend pound on a piece of wood with a hammer. Walk at least 100 long steps away from him. Now you can see him pounding on the wood, but the sound doesn't reach your ears until an instant afterwards. In fact, it takes about five seconds for sound to travel just one mile.

Light travels very fast. You can see lightning the moment that it happens. But sound travels much more slowly. Sometimes you have to wait and wait to hear the thunder. You can play a game with thunder and lightning. You can tell how far away the storm is. Count the seconds between the "flash and the crash." If you count more than five seconds, you know that the storm is over a mile away. If you count one or two seconds, then the storm is very close.

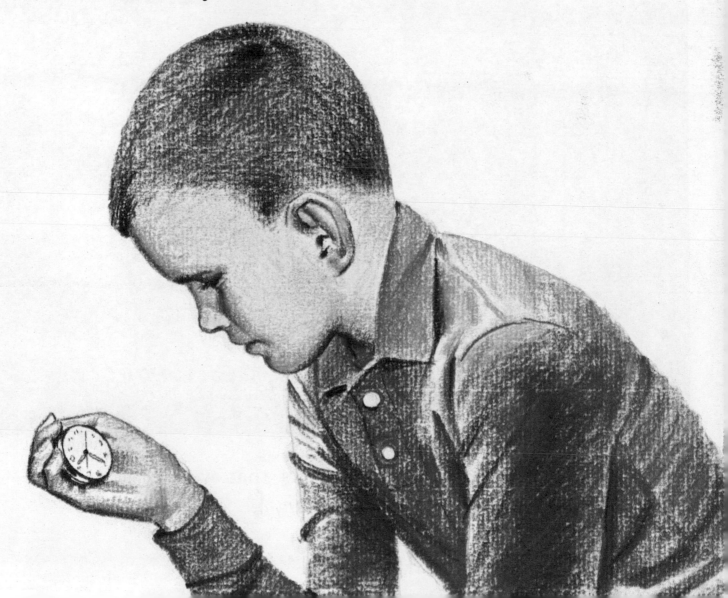

This is the kind of lightning that we see most often. It is called *streak lightning*.

This is called *fork lightning*. It looks like the roots
of a plant.

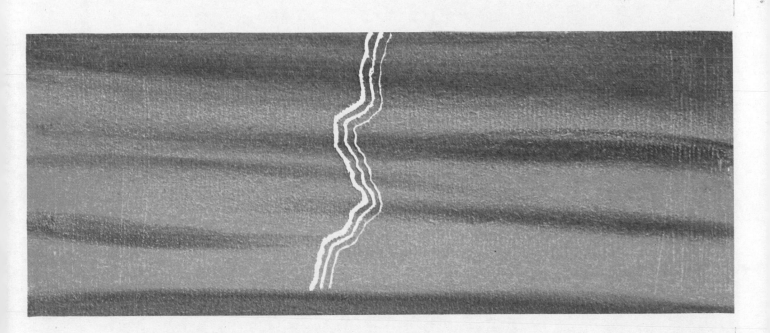

When lightning is blown sideways by the wind, it
is called *ribbon lightning*.

Sometimes we see a flashing glow of light low in the sky. This is *heat lightning*. It is no different than any other lightning, but the streak is too far away to be seen. And, because the storm is so far away, we can't hear the thunder.

There are hundreds and hundreds of thunder-storms all over the earth at this very minute. Is there a thunderstorm where you are?

ADDITIONAL INFORMATION ABOUT THUNDERSTORMS
(*for parents and teachers*)

FORMATION OF A THUNDERCLOUD: During warm fair weather, puffy cumulous clouds are a common sight in the sky. But a certain chain of events can quickly turn a cumulous cloud into a lofty turbulent cumulonimbus cloud, called a thundercloud.

Warm temperatures and water vapor in the air are two important ingredients needed to build a thundercloud. Heat from the land causes the moist air around it to expand and rise rapidly, creating "updrafts." When these warm currents rise to a high altitude where the air is cold, the water vapor condenses. It forms water droplets and/or ice crystals, and the cumulous cloud becomes bigger.

If the air is sufficiently unstable, then turbulent air currents will carry the water droplets to great heights and the top of the cloud will rise to seven or more miles where it flares off into an anvil-shaped top which is composed of very fine ice crystals.

The water droplets may join together and become large enough to fall from the cloud as rain, while some of the large drops will be carried to high elevations by the very strong vertical air currents within the thundercloud and join with ice crystals. These larger ice crystals will grow in size as they join other water droplets and freeze layer upon layer to form hailstones. Rain and hail will fall out of the cloud but frequently the hail melts before reaching the ground.

PRELUDE TO LIGHTNING: At the height of its fury, the thundercloud becomes a cauldron of colliding and opposing currents. As the billions of particles in the cloud rub and bang against each other, they become charged with electricity caused by the friction. Some parts of the cloud become positively charged, and other parts negatively charged.

The earth is also charged with electricity, the part beneath a thundercloud usually being positively charged. As these charges build up and the differential becomes high, the result is a discharge of electricity averaging 20 to 30 million volts.

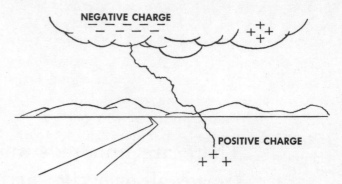

THE FLASH OF LIGHTNING: Lightning, then, can be thought of as a giant spark of electricity jumping between two oppositely charged bodies. It can take place in different parts of the same cloud, between two clouds, or between the cloud and earth.

The flash of lightning that we see is seldom one quick stroke from cloud to earth. A typical flash might proceed like this: The electric charge from the cloud reaches out toward the earth in a trail of halting steps. When this "stepped leader" gets close enough to the ground, the charge from the ground leaps up to meet it and travels back along the path toward the cloud. This is called the "return stroke" and produces the brilliant flash that we see. More leaders and return strokes may travel back and forth along this same path, but it all happens so quickly that we usually see it as a single flash.

FAST LIGHT—SLOW SOUND: Light travels at a speed of 186,000 miles per second and does not depend upon air for transmission. But there would be no sound without air. The source of a noise sets up sound waves which travel through the air to your ear. Compared to light, sound travels at a slow pace, averaging a little more than 1000 feet per second. This explains the time lapse between the flash of light and the clap of thunder from a distant storm.

THE SOUND OF THUNDER: Often thunder is heard as one loud crash, but sometimes we hear it crackle and rumble as well. This is easily understood when you keep in mind the fact that the "explosion" of hot expanded air is taking place all along the twisted path of the lightning. The noise from the part of the lightning nearest you will reach your ears first. The noise from the part farthest away from you reaches you last. Rumbling can also be the result of thunder echoing from the clouds or nearby hills.

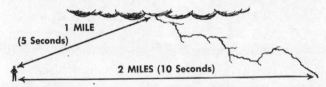

1 MILE (5 Seconds)

2 MILES (10 Seconds)

TYPES OF LIGHTNING: Lightning appears in many forms which can roughly be put into categories. In addition to the types described on pages 22–25, here are some other familiar ones: *Chain lightning,* also called *bead lightning,* begins as a streak and then appears to break up into bright dashes or "beads." *Sheet lightning* is much like heat lightning in that, instead of a streak, we see a glow of light in a broad area. The streak has happened inside of the thundercloud, and we see only the reflected or diffused light. *Ball lightning* is a rare and curious phenomenon that cannot be fully explained. It is a brilliant ball, usually a foot or more in diameter. It may appear to float at a leisurely speed through the air, across the ground, or through an open window before it finally dissipates.

WHERE LIGHTNING GOES: Cloud-to-earth lightning always takes the quickest and easiest path it can find to get to the ground. Air is a poor conductor of electricity. Thus, anything reaching up into the air, such as a tall tree, high building, or sailboat mast, offers an easier path.

When lightning reaches the ground, it continues to search out the best conductors, such as water, wet soil, or metal pipes. It then branches out in many directions until it loses its force.

Lightning rods are designed to attract lightning and keep it from hitting something else. The rods are grounded deep in the earth to conduct the charge safely away from the surface of the ground.

SAFETY PRECAUTIONS: Unsafe places during a thunderstorm are: wide open spaces, beaches, and hilltops where you could be the conductor. Stay away from trees and open water. It is safer not to touch electrical equipment, telephones, bathtubs, sinks, and the plumbing system in general, metal fences, pipes, and radiators. Any of these could carry a charge.

Safe places are: modern metal-frame buildings, buildings with lightning protection systems, trains, modern airplanes and ships, and steel-roofed automobiles, provided that you do not touch metal parts. These are all good conductors capable of carrying a big charge which will by-pass you.

THE FREQUENCY OF THUNDERSTORMS: The number of thunderstorms in any area depends greatly on the topography of the land and on local atmospheric conditions. The storms form most easily where sharp temperature contrasts create rapid updrafts, as in mountainous areas or along certain coastlines.

In the United States, Florida has more thunderstorms than any other state. The Midwestern states have frequent storms, sometimes appearing hand in hand with the dreaded tornadoes.

It has been estimated that about 44,000 thunderstorms occur around the world during the course of each day.

BEAD LIGHTNING

FORK LIGHTNING

SHEET LIGHTNING

HEAT LIGHTNING

STREAK LIGHTNING

RIBBON LIGHTNING

BALL LIGHTNING